A Response to War: Violet Oakley's World War II Triptychs

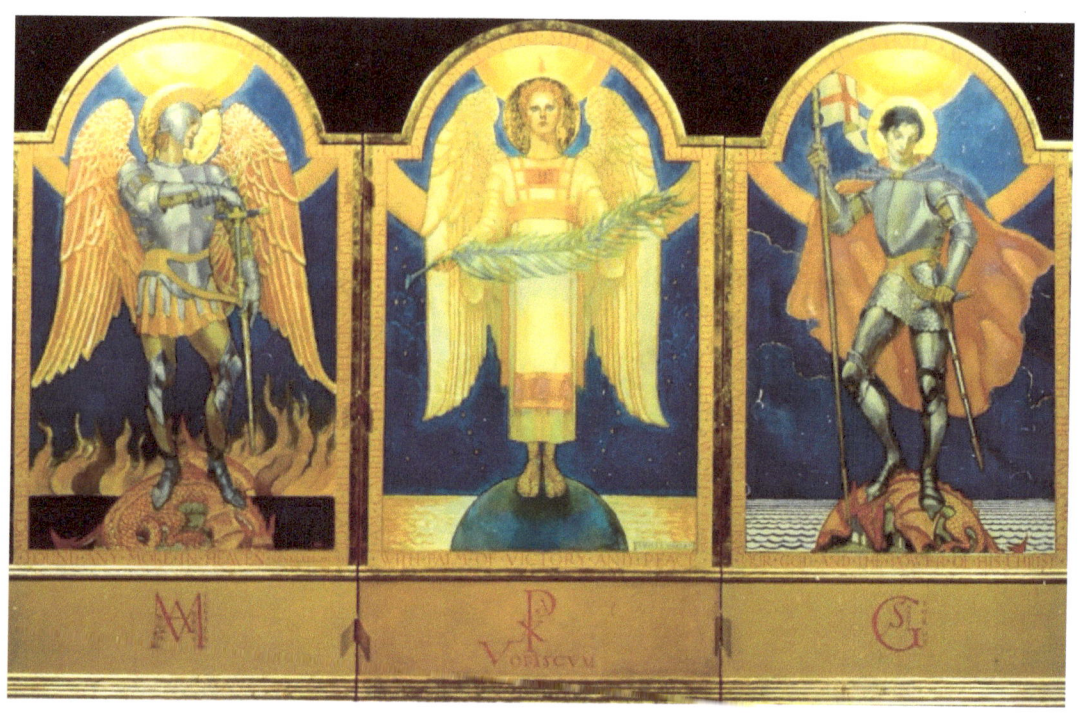

The Angels of Victory, 1942

Triptych No. 5

A Response to War:

Violet Oakley's World War II Triptychs

for The Citizens Committee

for the Army and Navy, Inc.

by Jane DuPree Richardson

Gray Oak Books

ISBN: 9780941062275

Published by:
Gray Oak Books
PO Box 404
Apalachicola, FL 32329

Front Cover: Saint George, *The Angels of Victory*, 1942. (Delaware Art Museum)

Back Cover: Goliath, *David and Goliath*, 1945. (Woodmere Art Museum)

Frontispiece: *Angels of Victory*, 1942. L. to R. Saint Michael, Archangel; Saint Gabriel, Archangel; Saint George. (Delaware Art Museum)

Madonna of the Sea, Triptych No. 165, courtesy of the William Benton Museum of Art, University of Connecticut, Storrs.

Christ Walking on the Water, Triptych No. 242, courtesy The Philadelphia Museum of Art.

Maquette for *Madonna of the Crusaders, 1942*, courtesy Pennsylvania Academy of the Fine Arts Museum. All pencil and ink studies courtesy Pennsylvania Academy of the Fine Arts Museum.

All other illustrations, unless otherwise credited, are courtesy of the Archives of American Artists, The Smithsonian Institute, Washington, D.C.

Contents

To Dr. Patricia Likos Ricci

Without her continuing support and advice

I would never have finished this small book.

I value her friendship.

Introduction

In 2003, I was invited to act as curator of an exhibition of the works of Violet Oakley by Dr. Valerie Livingston then Head of the Art Department and Director of the Lore Degenstein Gallery at Susquehanna University in Pennsylvania. I was Director of the Northumberland County Historical Society in Sunbury, just across the River and had curated a very successful exhibition of Pennsylvania German crafts and life style two years before. All I knew about Violet Oakley was that she was the artist who had painted the murals for the Pennsylvania State Capitol in Harrisburg.

During my preliminary research, I became especially interested in a small segment of Oakley's enormous output—her World War II Triptychs. For one reason, I myself had served on active duty as a WAVE officer during the first Korea, and had attended many religious services in base Chapels and plain rooms designated for religious services of any and all Faiths. I wanted to see what Oakley had painted for such rooms.

The second reason for my interest was that Oakley's religious art intrigued me, since she was a convert to and practitioner of Christian Science, a denomination that does not use works of art in its buildings or publications. My father was a practicing Christian Scientist. As a child and teenager I attended Sunday School with my brother and mother at the First Baptist Church, then we all went to a rented room with my father for a Christian Scientist service with the small number of dedicated followers who would read together.

For these reasons, I, a convert to Roman Catholicism and an admirer of the great art of that faith, felt that I needed to explore Oakley's triptychs in more detail. It has been very rewarding.

I have done my best, trying to track down all Oakley's triptychs, but I leave it to younger scholars to continue the search. Any errors in this book are mine.

Jane DuPree Richardson

Apalachicola, Florida

December 2018

A Response to War:
Violet Oakley's World War II Triptychs

Citizens Committee for the Army and Navy, Inc.

36 EAST 36th STREET, NEW YORK 16, N. Y.

Telephone: MUrray Hill 3-5366

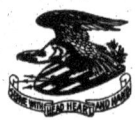

Will you send a triptych (altar panels) to a Post, a Base, a Ship or Unit of our armed forces?

We have a long list of requests and new requests daily.

We **must** fill them immediately.

Prominent American Artists from all over the country are working on this in the spirit of service and for token payments.

Will you avail yourself of the privilege, making possible one of these lovely panels for religious services wherever the request may be?

The large volume of requests has made it necessary to make immediately four editions of one hundred each of the four most asked for designs.

This work serves Art, Religion and the Armed Forces and is an unspoken message from us at home to those defending our civilization.

<u>PLEDGE</u>

I will give a triptych - $350.00 ....
I will give 5 triptychs -$1,750.00 ....

Name ....
Address ....

<u>DONATIONS</u>

Donations to the Triptych Fund in any amount will be most welcome.

<u>PLEDGE</u>

I will give an Edition of 100 Reproductions - $5,000.00 (in color on full size panel of the original)

Name ....
Address ....

I would like the inscription to be:

Name of donor to be inscribed on panel or panels.

<u>PLEDGE</u>

I will donate $...............

Name ....

Address ....

I.

The Citizens Committee for the Army and Navy, Inc.

The Citizens Committee for the Army and Navy, Inc. (hereafter CCAN) was formed in 1940 by a group of civilians and military officers concerned by the threat posed by the anticipated outbreak of war in Europe. Its purpose was to meet the first emergency needs of the Selective Service. The Committee undertook to convey to the country's fighting forces the best of the art, literature, music and science of Western Civilization for their relaxation, recreation, and intellectual resource. Sub-committees were formed to deal with requests for furniture for commons rooms, stage curtains, sports equipment and trophies, radios, music and musical instruments, paintings, photographs, and volunteer entertainment. The Committee tried to fulfill any request from the services, even frequently unusual ones, such as knitted goods and cigarettes. This included requests for altar paintings known as triptychs.[1]

A Need for Sacred Spaces

The call for triptychs began in response to appeals from the fighting men themselves. Chaplains who lived with them and led them in worship sensed the need for a church atmosphere in services on land, sea and on the battlefield. Triptychs provided the answer.[2] These easily transportable works of religious art were requested by combatants of all faiths, and chaplains received altars where there were no chapels. They installed them or carried them into whatever space could be found, whether chapel, barracks, ship, bivouac or on a battle wagon.

From the beginning, ranking officers of the Armed Forces, together with civil and religious leaders of all faiths supported this non-denominational civilian group organized to help chaplains care for the spiritual needs of the fighting men. The Triptych Movement became one of the most prominent and publicly visible of the offerings of the CCAN, which later cooperated with the American Academy in Rome (hereafter AAR).[3]

Many people helped to make possible this giving to service men the spiritual life they wanted, but one person in particular became the dominant force behind it. That person was Mrs. Junius Spencer Morgan Jr., wife of the eldest son of J. P. Morgan, who became head of this noted financial firm at the death of his father.[4] Louise Converse, daughter of composer Frederick Converse, had grown up in staid Boston society. In accordance with the tradition of the famous family into which she married, she had always avoided any activity which might bring her into the public eye. However, in 1940, when the National Guard became the frame of the growing Army, and the United States was beginning to mobilize, an organization in New York came into being to provide recreational equipment for the state's Twenty-seventh Division. Mrs. Morgan joined it and became a founding member. She could not have anticipated that it would eventually be incorporated as the Citizens Committee for the Army and Navy, Inc. , and that she would be leaving her home every morning for an office and lunching at a desk. But her husband was preparing to go on active duty in the United States Navy, and everybody was needed. Private lives no longer counted very much.

Mrs. Morgan was known as an energetic, intense woman and became one of the chief executives of the Committee, with a special interest in the Triptych sub-committee. She worked closely throughout the war years with Barry Faulkner, who was at that time director of the AAR which had moved its offices to New York City for the duration.[5]

Barry Faulkner (1881-1966) was born in Keene, New Hampshire and became an artist primarily known for his murals. He was a student of his cousin, the naturalist painter, Abbott H. Thayer, and was sometimes called the "father of camouflage".

In 1907, Barry Faulkner became the first American artist to receive the prestigious Prix de Rome from the American Academy there. Prior to World War I, he organized artists who wanted to serve as camouflage experts into a unit called the New York Camouflage Society, and he served with the Army's American Camouflage Corps in France. His main achievements throughout his life were as a muralist with works in many well-known public buildings in New York City and throughout the country. During World War II, he served as director of the AAR in its wartime headquarters in New York City.[6]

Faulkner and Mrs. Morgan had a close working relationship with regular meetings, frequent phone conversations, and numerous written communications. Together, they administered a roster of over 300 artists who agreed to paint triptychs for the modest fee of $250. (This amount was increased as the War lengthened). They included Donald DeLue, Edith Emerson, Hildreth Meiere, Violet Oakley, Frank Reilly, Frank H. Schwarz, and Nina Barr Wheeler. Faulkner and Mrs. Morgan also organized extensive publicity for the Triptych project in military and news publications. They created a movement to enlist art students throughout the country to enter competitions with their own works and ideas, and offered prizes for the best. They encouraged exhibitions of the triptychs after their completion by the artist and before being sent to their destinations with the armed forces. Notably among these were an exhibition at the National Academy of Design in New York City in October 1942, where Christmas cards of the triptychs were sold to raise funds, and a large exhibition at the Woodmere Art Gallery (now the Woodmere Art Museum) in Chestnut Hill, Pennsylvania. One or more of Violet Oakley's triptychs were included in each of these.[7]

In addition, triptychs as they were finished were on continuous exhibition at the Headquarters of the Committee for the Army and Navy, 36 East 36th Street, New York, Monday through Friday, 10 am to 5 pm, with the greeting, "All are invited."

In the realm of newspaper publicity, articles were regularly carried by *The New York Times*, *The Philadelphia Enquirer*, and the *Bar Harbor Times*. In the latter, Mary Roberts Rinehart, well-known author of suspense and mystery novels, contributed a small but encouraging piece referencing a revival in the belief in miracles as men of all faiths prayed at make-shift altars.[8] Mrs. Morgan herself contributed an article for "THINK Magazine" in December 1943, explaining the purpose of the triptych project and mentioning some of the many responses the Committee had received from chaplains and enlisted personnel in the various services.[9]

The Artists and the Materials

Designed to be portable, each triptych consisted of three panels. A full size triptych measured about 4 x 6 feet when open, and 4 x 3 feet when the wing sections were folded toward the center. Detailed blueprints showed

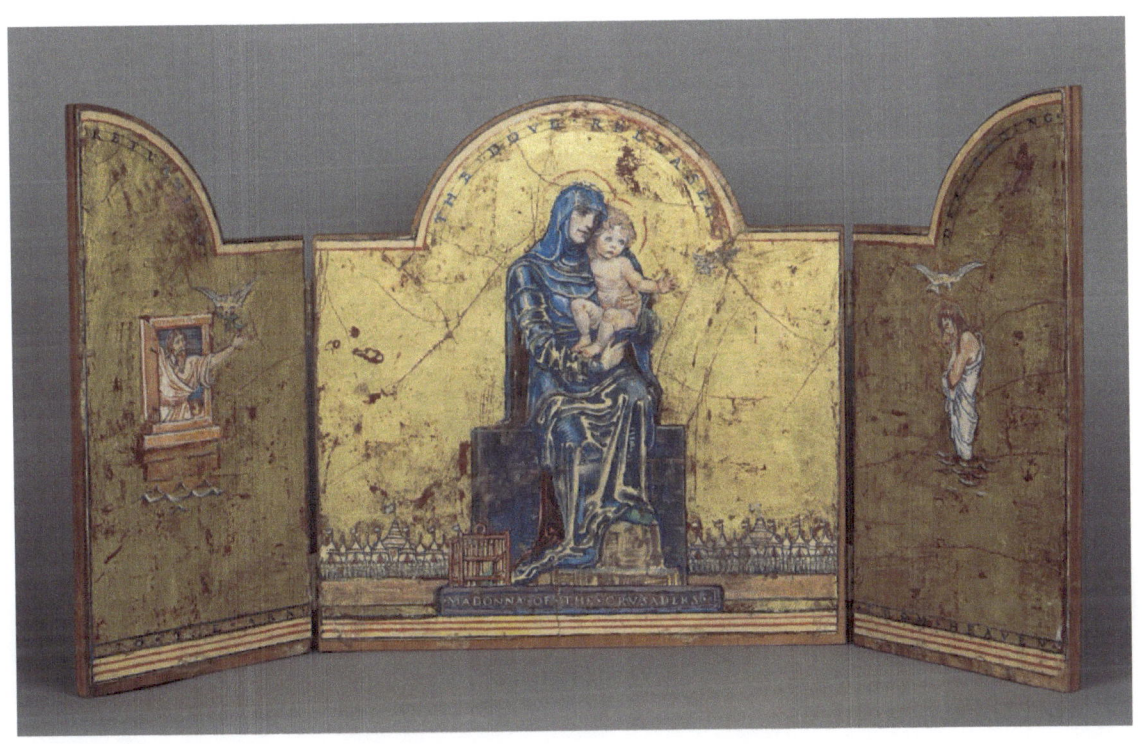

Maquette for *Madonna of the Crusaders, 1942*
Triptych No. 42

the various forms that could be used for the top of the triptych: straight, curved or pointed. In this compact manner, they could be set up quickly wherever men were fighting. These were prepared in advance in accordance with service requirements, those for the Army, the Army Air

Force, and Naval land bases were made of weatherproof plywood. Those for naval ships at sea were made of bullet- and fire-proof steel.[10]

Inspired by the gift to one of the new battleships, Violet Oakley's "Christ Stilling the Storm" for the *USS Seattle* in 1942, chaplains realized that portable altars could carry comfort and strength to those charged with the overwhelming task of defending this country and preserving its future.

When fighting forces learned that these portable altars were available, the Committee was inundated with requests. By December 1944, according to Hallowell V. Morgan, Secretary of the Philadelphia Triptych Committee, over 600 requests had been received, and more than 300 altars had been distributed to military posts and naval bases in thirty-seven states, as well as more than twenty bases overseas, and to military and naval units engaging the enemy on all fronts. By serving as a spiritual focus, a triptych made it possible for a chaplain to minister in an atmosphere of beauty and dignity.[11]

Once a request was received, it was reviewed and a design was selected by a committee of nationally known artists and architects. The artist receiving the commission was required to submit a full-scale sketch

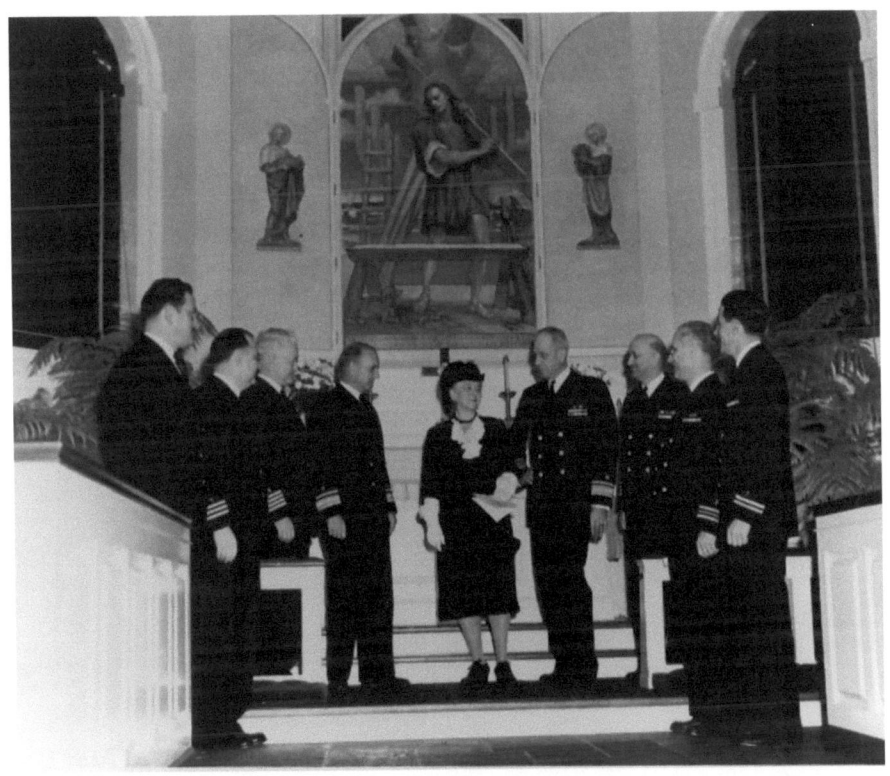

Violet Oakley and naval officers at the dedication of her triptych altarpiece *Christ the Carpenter* at the Philadelphia Naval Base Chapel, circa 1944.

to the jury, which approved it before it was painted. The finished product was then delivered to the Armed Forces.

At the time, this movement was hailed as the most important art program to come out of the war by Chaplain Rear-Admiral William H. Thomas, USN. In donating these triptychs, individuals and groups on the home front found the opportunity to give something of spiritual value directly to the fighting men. Those paying the full cost of a Triptych could have it inscribed as a tribute or memorial and select the unit or ship to which it would be sent. It could also bear the name of the donor. The committee kept a registry of every triptych and its disposition. It was agreed that if the triptych survived the war and was no longer needed by the unit to which it was assigned, the committee would make an appropriate disposition in accordance with the wishes of the donor.[12]

The Triptych Then and Now

The history of portable triptychs is long and memorable. In the Middle Ages they were "paintings executed on three compartments or panels, so constructed that the two wings may fold on hinges over the center." Some well-known examples include the Staelot portable altar, made to contain two small Byzantine reliquaries of the True Cross, ca. 1154.[13] From the 14th to the 16th centuries, triptychs played an important role in the religious life of the Italian, Germanic and Flemish States, and are among the most outstanding art works of these periods.[14]

Would the triptych be the form of choice in today's modern warfare? "No," says Chaplain Col. George L. Reed, USA-Ret. He agreed that such an enhancement would be welcome in established chapels on land bases, but would not now be of use for chaplains assigned to duty in a war zone. When he served as a Protestant chaplain in the 1990s, he was given a wooden container a little larger than a shoe box, painted olive drab, that contained a communion set, an altar cloth, candles, a Bible stand and a cross. Appropriate items were in the kits of other denominations. Today's chaplain is issued two compact kits each the size of a cell phone that fit onto the belt, again containing items appropriate to the religion represented by the chaplain.[15] All chaplains must minister to any and all service personnel, whether or not the chaplain's religion is a match. Initially, chaplains were all Protestant ministers. As of 2006, more than 200 religions have been granted ecclesiastical endorsement by the Department of Defense, including the Buddhist, Catholic, Jewish, Mormon, and Muslim faiths.[16] Today, constantly getting in and out of helicopters to be taken where needed, the chaplain is more portable than anything he or she can be issued. The Triptych Movement of World War II was a unique artistic endeavor.

II.

A Response to War: Violet Oakley's World War II Triptychs

Violet Oakley (1874-1961) was one of over 300 artists to answer the call from the CCAN. The only woman acclaimed as a member of the American Renaissance mural movement, Oakley lived in Philadelphia and is best known for her murals in the Pennsylvania State Capitol in Harrisburg, Pennsylvania. However, these public works represent only a part of her prodigious output. In a career of over sixty years, Oakley created murals and stained glass designs for church interiors, schools, civic buildings and private residences. She also illustrated books and magazines, designed posters, painted and drew hundreds of portraits, and made sketches of her travels.[17] Oakley's work as a muralist and illustrator has been well documented, but her work for the CCAN has remained obscure. This may be due to the fact that the location of most of her triptychs remains unknown. This paper represents the work I have done searching for a few of the triptychs Oakley produced for CCAN and the AAR.

Oakley's participation in the project might appear unexpected. She rose to fame in the early 20th century as the first woman to receive a public commission: the murals decorating the Pennsylvania State Capitol Building. Her study of William Penn and the Quakers, plus the influence

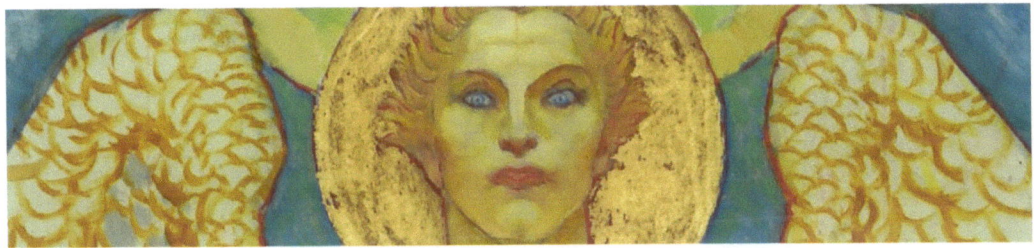

Detail from *The Angels of Victory.*

of Jane Addams and the Women's International League for Peace and Freedom[18] converted Oakley to pacifism with ideals of universal brotherhood, freedom of religion , and the establishment of a world court of arbitration to supplant wars. Nonetheless, influenced by the two World Wars that occurred during her lifetime, she loaned her art to the quest for peace and became a tireless advocate for international government, first for the League of Nations, and later for the United Nations. During World War I, Oakley designed posters for War Bonds to aid the war effort. In 1949, she attended a meeting of the Moral Rearmament Society in Geneva, Switzerland.

It is not clear how Oakley got involved with the CCAN, possibly through the Philadelphia Triptych Committee.[19] In any case, she was a contributor from the beginning and started painting triptychs in 1941.

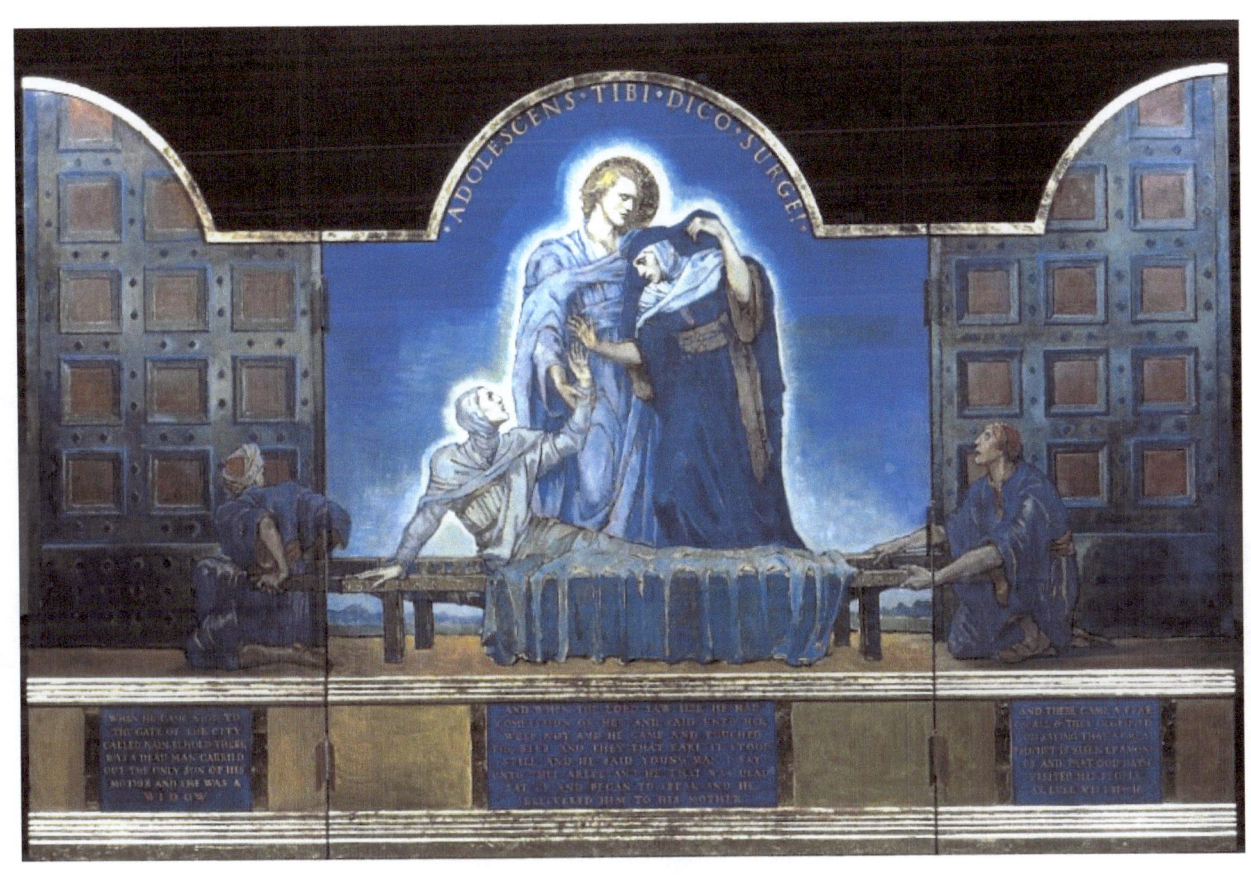

And He That Was Dead Sat Up, 1944
Triptych No. 166

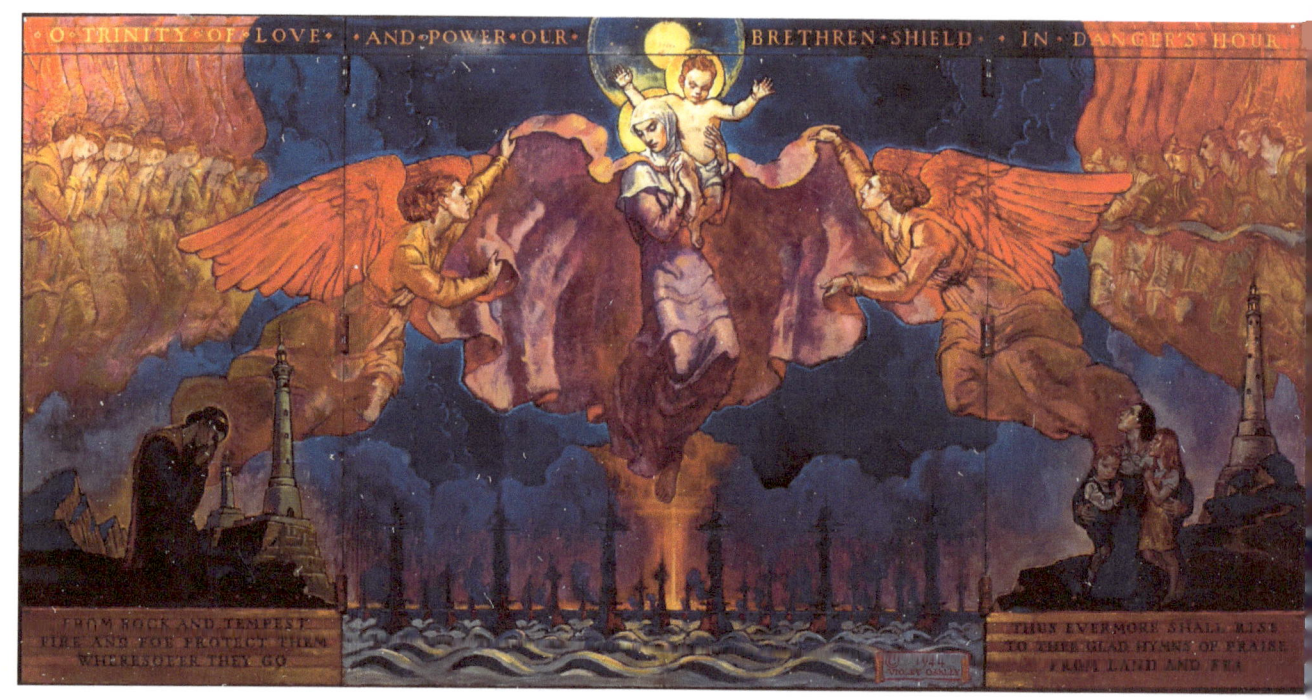

Madonna of the Sea, 1943
Triptych No. 165

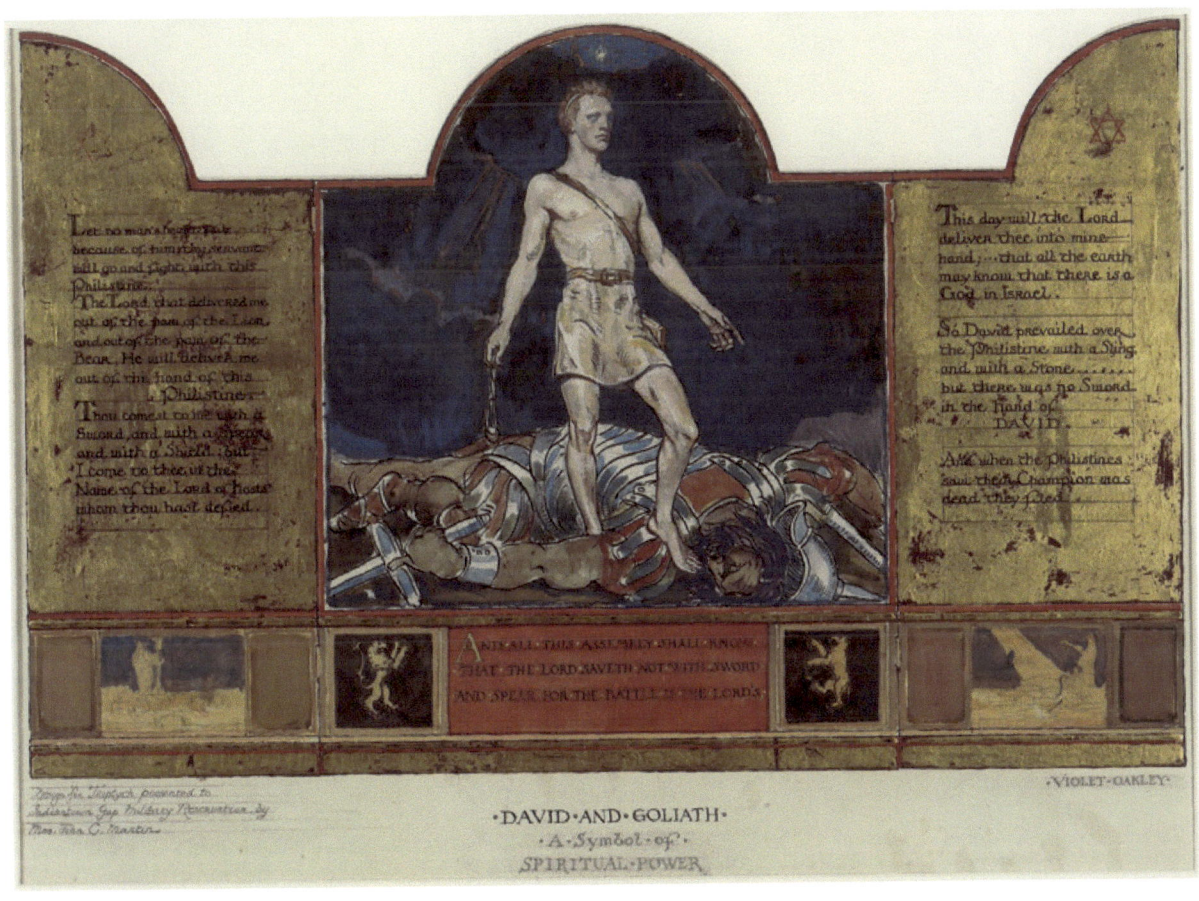

Study for *David and Goliath*, 1945
Triptych No. 250

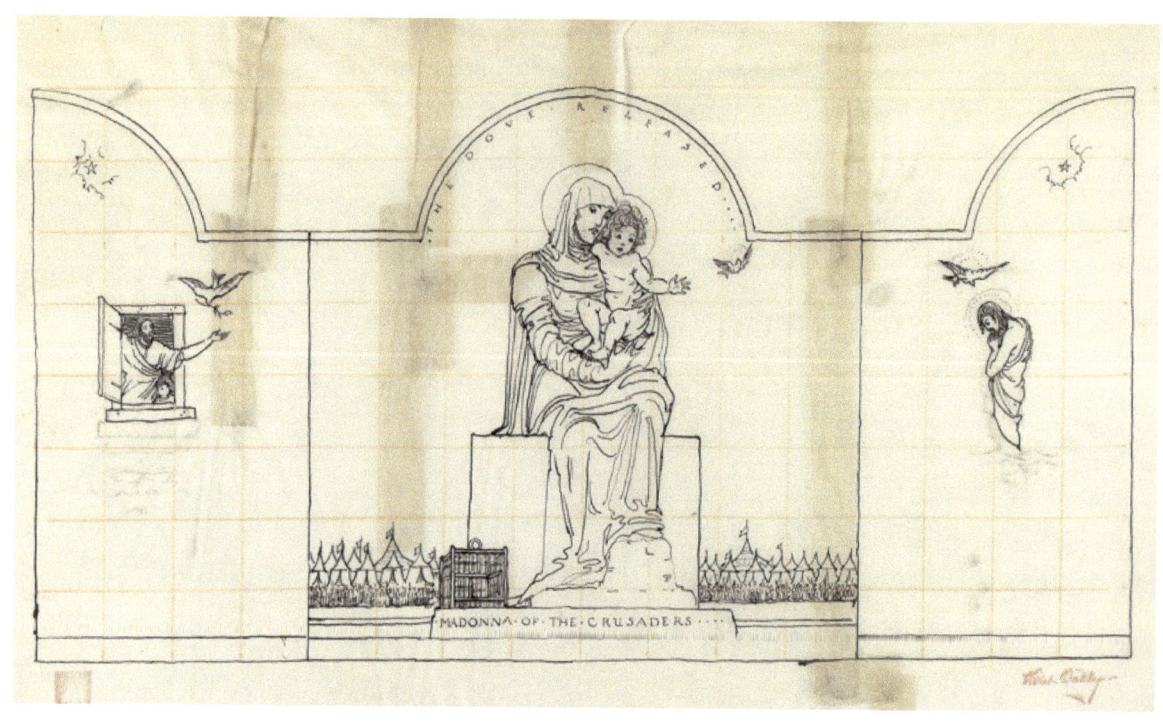

Study for *Madonna of the Crusaders*
Triptych No. 42

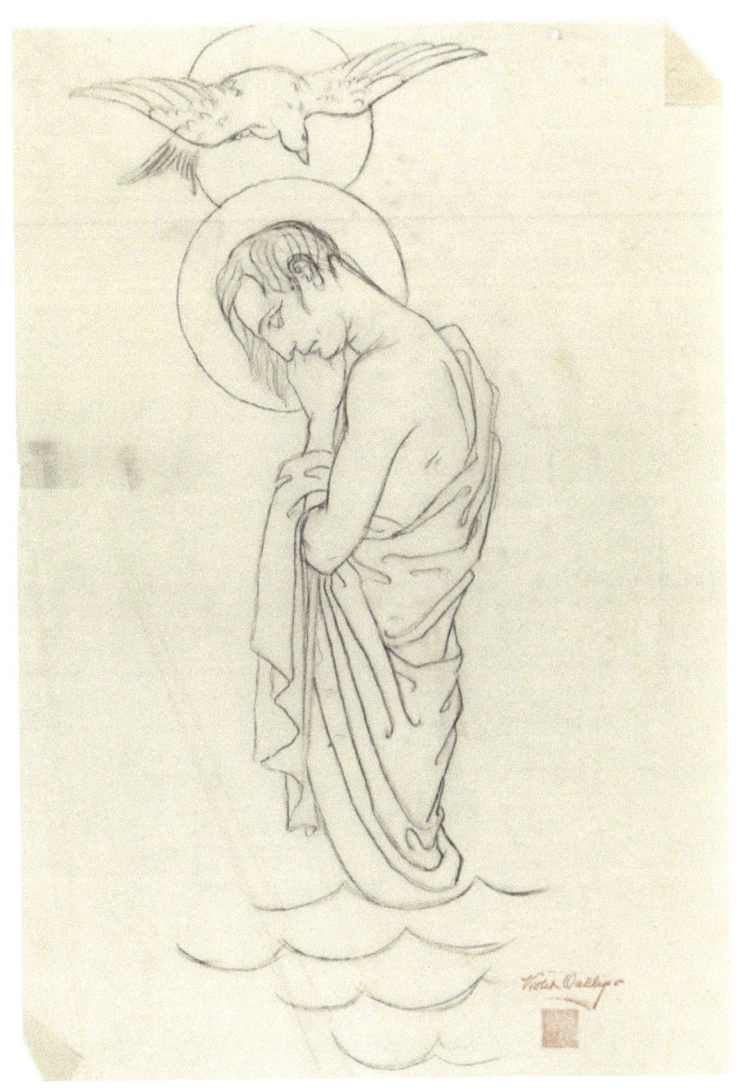

Study for *Madonna of the Crusaders (right panel)*

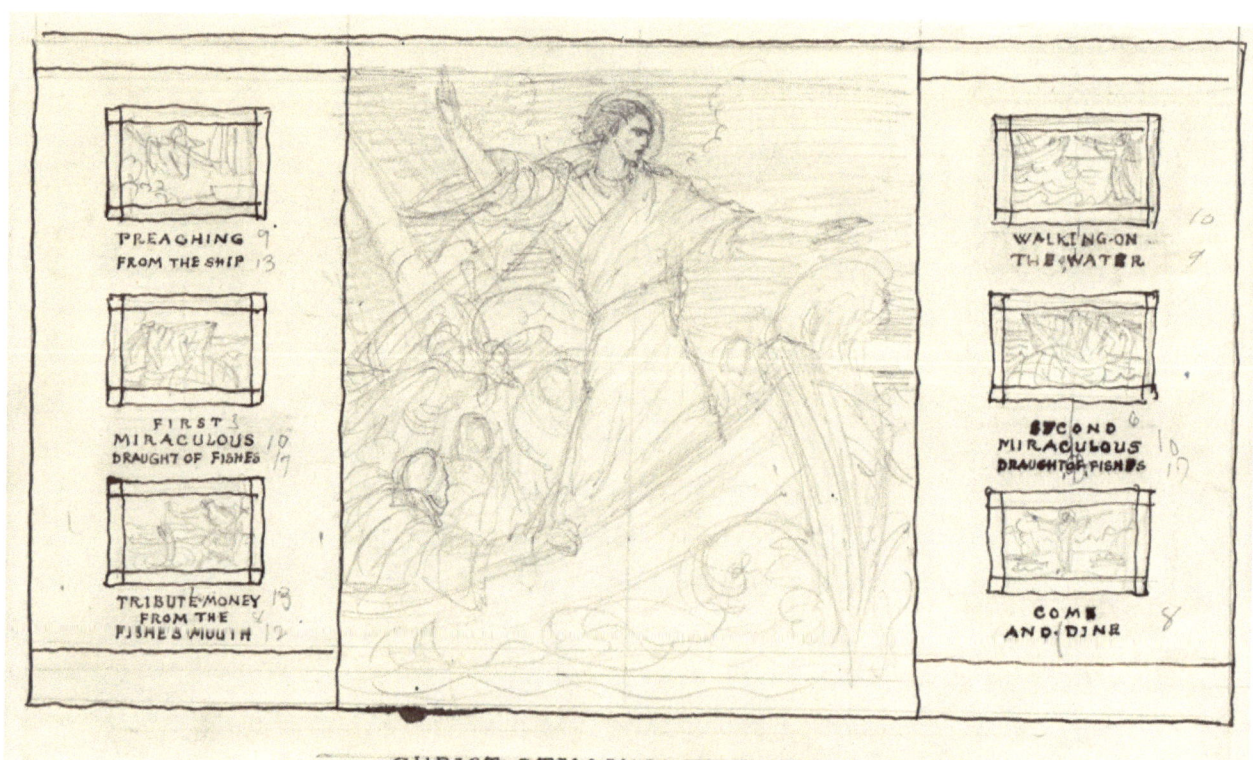

Study for *Christ Stilling the Storm*
Triptych No. 189

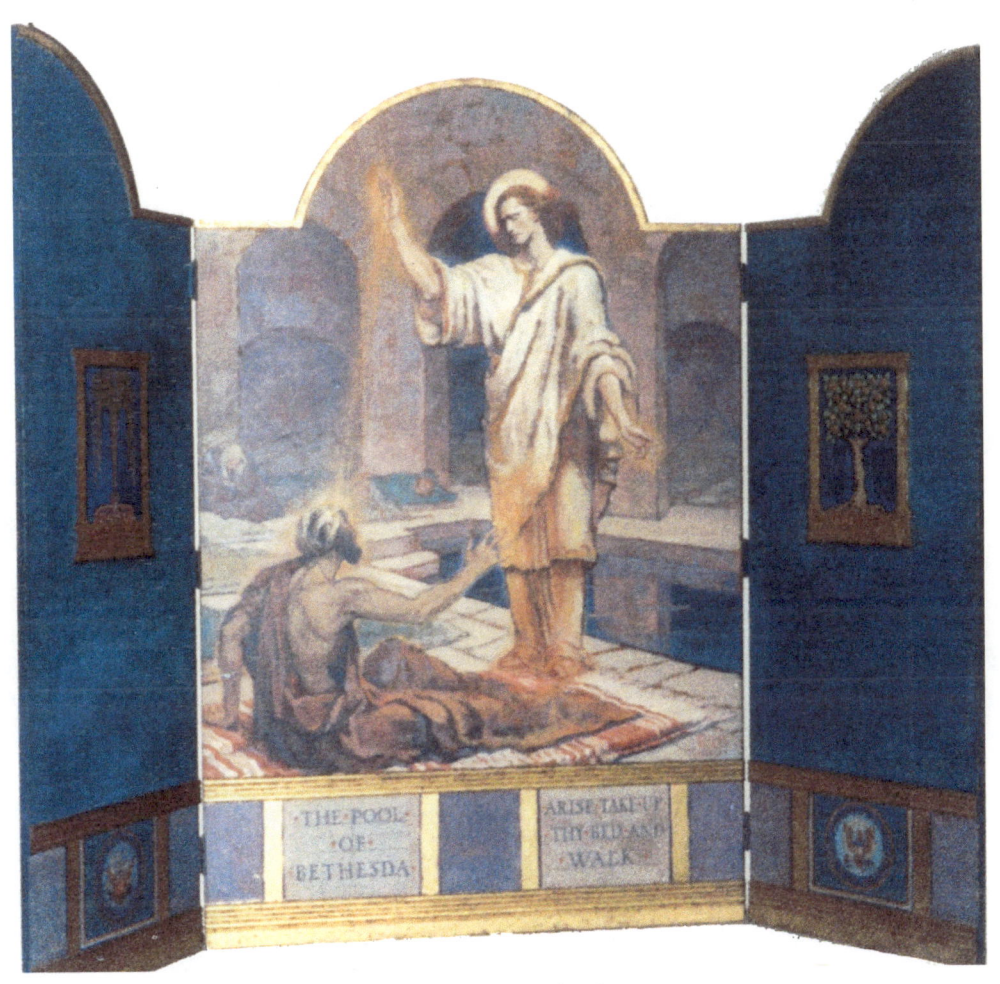

The Pool of Bethesda
Triptych No. 279

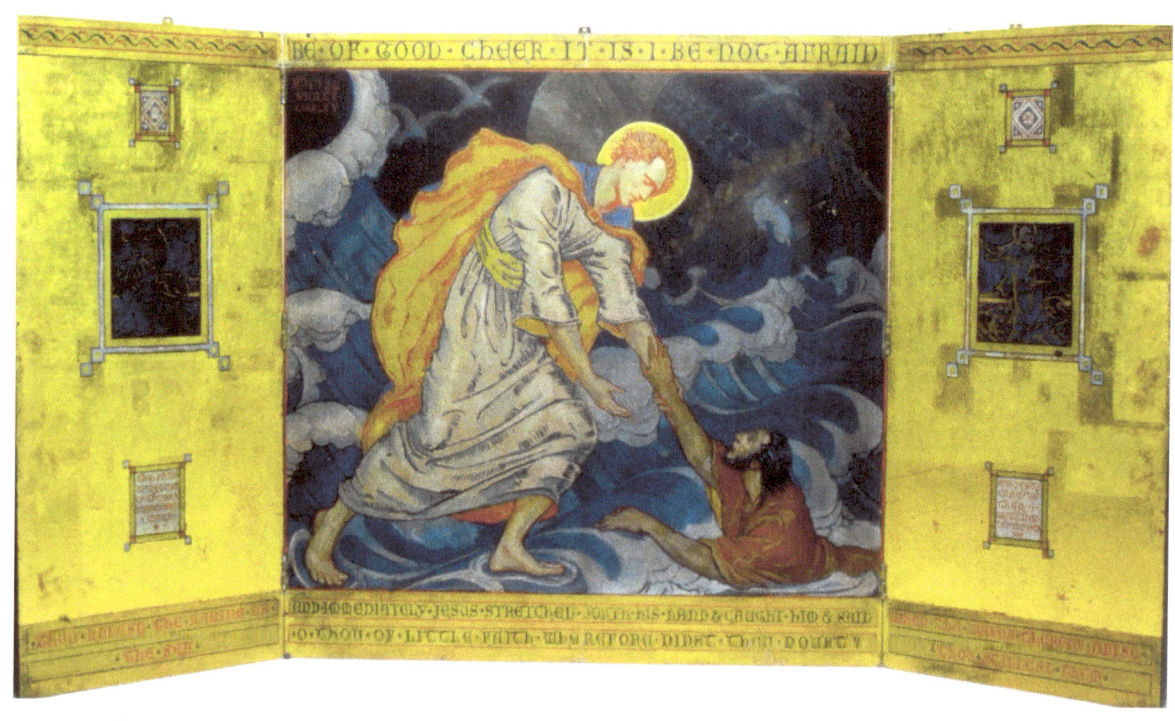

Christt Walking on the Water
Triptych No. 242

The World War II Triptych Movement

During World War II, Oakley was one of many artists who painted portable triptych altar pieces for the Armed Services. Between 1942 and 1945, she was commissioned by the CCAN to paint twenty-four for use on war ships and in chapels on military bases. During that period, some of the triptychs were exhibited at the Corcoran Gallery, Washington, D.C.; the Woodmere Art Gallery (now the Woodmere Art Museum), Philadelphia, December 1943 through January 1944; the National Academy of Design, October 1945; and the New York Headquarters of the Citizens Committee for the Army and Navy, September 1945.

Violet Oakley and the Triptych Form

Violet Oakley's use of the triptych throughout her artistic career indicated an affinity for the form. As a student, she visited and studied art during her first trip to France and Italy in 1894-1895, where triptychs were a common form of earning points in Heaven by hiring an artist to paint a

Holy picture with the donor and his wife depicted praying on one of the wings. She returned to Florence in 1905, where she was deeply moved at seeing the Domenico Ghirlandaio fresco, "Madonna of Mercy", ca. 1472. She later admitted that this fresco served as inspiration for the "Unity" figure in her mural for the Senate Chamber in the Pennsylvania State Capitol.[20]

In the murals she created for the Senate Chamber of the Pennsylvania State Capitol in 1917, we see her development of the triptych form. The main panel shows the central figure of "Unity", flanked by soldiers beating their swords into ploughshares on the left panel, and Dante, Jane Addams and The People on the right panel. In 1924 she created the triptych entitled "The Great Wonder: A Vision of the Apocalypse," for the Vassar College Alumnae House Living Room[21] in memory of her sister Hester Oakley Ward, class of 1891. The central Madonna and Child also served as the inspiration for Oakley's World War II triptychs, "Madonna of the Crusaders" and "Madonna of the Sea." In 1929, Oakley completed the "Life of Moses", an altar reredos (a decorated panel that stands directly behind the altar) for the Fleisher Art Memorial in Philadelphia. It is one unit in the form of a 12-panel "vita " icon, popular in the Orthodox tradition. The central figure is the Egyptian princess holding the infant Moses, a reference to the Renaissance Madonna and Child. She is flanked by scenes from the life of Moses.[22]

In her last public commission, the murals "Great Women of the Bible Series" for the First Presbyterian Church in Germantown, Pennsylvania, Oakley painted the central figure of the Archangel Jophiel over a doorway, flanked by Eve receiving the apple from the serpent on the left, and the Virgin Mary welcoming a supplicant on the right. These have recently been removed and packed away as the Church has now been closed.[23]

The Art and Artistry of Violet Oakley

Although discipleship is the dominant characterization of the work of Violet Oakley, her genius lies in the selection of the influences that permitted her to develop her own style. Oakley's teacher and mentor, the illustrator Howard Pyle, stressed the search for the inner feeling of each person in an illustration, which entitled the illustrator to bring spirituality to her work. Pyle gave his students permission to follow their intent to imbue figures with an inner spirit and personal energy, but he did not guide them to paint like him, though many of his students did just that. Oakley drew proudly from Pyle and worked developing her skills in drawing and painting. Her originality lay in the force of an inner spirit that permitted her to fuse the visual elements of two periods of art history: the Early Renaissance and the Pre-Raphaelites. This is especially true in her World War II triptychs.

From the Early Renaissance, Oakley brings the tableau of the altar, a limited space indicated by overlapping shapes rather than by elaborate perspective. She used this form in much of her work and was temperamentally and artistically ready to paint the portable altars for the World War II Triptychs, created for the CCAN.

In her work, Oakley utilized the stylized pallet of such early Renaissance painters as Giotto, Fra Angelico, and Paolo and Giovanni Veneziano, artists who painted religious frescos and murals. In her World War II triptychs, Oakley used color in large monochromatic fields, for instance a dramatic red, painted with pigments toned only by hue and shade, not by other colors; or a vivid blue, which stands alone without any need to relate it to its surroundings by integrating neighboring colors.

Instead of using the color dabbing methods of the artists of the Impressionist Movement, such as Monet, she followed the Pre-Raphaelites, who chose to idealize nature, and strove for beauty at the expense of reality; it epitomized innocence, purity and spirituality.[24] Like Pre-Raphaelite paintings, Oakley's figures and faces are given bold outlines, a treatment she learned from Howard Pyle. All figures, male and female alike, are given graceful physiques and long tapering hands. These methods can be seen in her World War II triptychs.

III.

Conclusion

Fortunately for this study, both the CCAN and the AAR kept extensive records of the art work prepared during the Triptych Movement. Both of these are now housed in the Archives of American Artists, the Smithsonian Institute, Washington, D. C. Oakley also kept a record of the triptychs she prepared for the Committee, though it is incomplete, and the recipient of the triptychs is sketchy. It is included in her papers, also at the AAA.

Of the various listings of Oakley's triptychs, I consider the "Artist" list, included in the main folder under the artist's name in the AAR files to be the most reliable. Even though it does not give the titles of the triptychs, it does give a break-down of the disposition of each one. In some cases, a triptych was transferred sequentially to several locations. Interestingly, seventeen of Oakley's twenty-four triptychs were given to Naval ships or bases. During World War II, the Philadelphia Naval Base and Shipyard was one of the largest in the country.[25] This could be the reason for the early establishment of the Philadelphia Triptych Committee which possibly directed her triptychs to Naval installations. Ten Oakley triptychs were turned over to a Milton (sic) Horwitz on 12 May 1974, nearly thirty years after the end of World War II. Three of those are now known to be in museum collections. Also, as far as is known, the triptych "Christ at the Pool of Bethesda" is the only Oakley triptych still in the location where it was dedicated, the Bethesda Naval Hospital. I can only surmise that the triptychs turned over to Mr. Horowitz were among those that survived the war and, no longer needed by the units to which they were assigned, were disposed of by the Committee in accordance with the wishes of the donor as agreed.[26]

In any case, these four Triptychs are the only ones I have been able to locate, though I have tried to track down others. The only response to queries was from the United States Naval Academy in Annapolis. The Commanding Officer at that time had never seen it, and the Curator of the Museum had not seen nor heard of it in the forty years he had been there. However, the Curator did send me a copy of the 1945 issue of *Shipmate Magazine* with the article by Rear Admiral Chaplin William H. Thomas.

In the numbering assigned by the CCAN, No. 5, "The Angels of Victory," is in the collections of the Delaware Art Museum, DAM #1975.129.[27] Originally sent to Floyd Bennett Field, New York, it was donated to the Delaware Art Museum in 1975 by Joseph Flom and Martin(sic) Horwitz. No. 242, "Christ Walking on the Water," originally donated to the USS Cebu, is in the collections of the Philadelphia Museum of Art, accession number 1975.180.1. It also was donated to the Museum in 1975 by Joseph Flom and Martin (sic) Horwitz. Likewise, "The Madonna of the Sea," No. 165, originally sent to the USS Baltimore, was donated to the William Benton Museum of Art at the University of Connecticut, where it still remains.

The present whereabouts of the other seven triptychs given to Milton or Martin Horwitz is unknown.

In studying the "Artist" list, I felt that of all the land locations for Oakley's triptychs, the one that I might be able to check out myself was the Bethesda Naval Hospital, which received Triptych No. 279, "The Pool of Bethesda," on 9 March 1945. At first I was unable to make a visit, so I sent my friends Mary Ann and Bill Wren to search for it. They found it, *in situ,* still in the nook in the entry foyer to the Hospital Chapel, where it had been installed in 1945. After I visited the Hospital in 2004 and made arrangements for the United States Navy to loan this triptych, it became the centerpiece for the Oakley Exhibition which I curated for the Lore Degenstein Gallery at Susquehanna University, Selinsgrove, Pennsylvania, in 2005. It was the first time it had ever been exhibited in a museum.

The Drexel Collection, Drexel University, Philadelphia, has gouache and watercolor drawings for two Oakley triptychs: No. 23, "Christ Stilling the Storm," Drexel #5357, and No. 166, "The Widow of Nain," Drexel #5358. The Woodmere Art Museum, Chestnut Hill, Philadelphia, has a charcoal and white chalk drawing of the giant Goliath, used for triptych No. 250, "David and Goliath," the only one for which Oakley used an Old Testament subject.

Oakley simplified her designs as she continued to create her triptychs. The first "Angels of Victory," "Christ Stilling the Storm," "The Madonna of the Crusaders," "The Madonna of the Sea" and "The Widow of Nain" all have a design that covers the three sections of the triptych. Later ones, such as "David and Goliath", "The Pool of Bethesda", "Christ the Carpenter", and the last two of "Christ Stilling the Storm," completed by Edith Emerson, have a strong center panel that tells the entire story, but the wings carry only a brief supporting text consisting of military seals or donor information that stand alone. Oakley also used some designs more than once. There are two "Angels of Victory," six "Christ Stilling the Storm," four "Widow of Nain," five "Madonna of the Sea," two "Madonna of the Crusaders," and two of "Christ Walking on the Water." "David and Goliath," "The Madonna of the Ship," "Christ at the Pool of Bethesda," and "Christ the Carpenter" are the only unique designs. In this case, it should be remembered that military units were able to request a preferred design.

Oakley was deeply spiritual. Raised in the Episcopal Faith, she converted to Christian Science in 1900, and later filled the position of Second Reader, the person who supplies readings from the Bible to complement selections from Mary Baker Eddy's *Science and Health with Key to the Scriptures* by the First Reader.[28] There are no ordained ministers or pastors. Oakley wrote of herself: "Religion, non-sectarian religion, has been and still is the most important thing in my life. Realizing that painting has always been one of the clearest expositions of the religious spirit and realizing that religion has been the inspiration of most of the significant painting in the world, I felt that I had received a sacred challenge. I told myself throughout the years, daily, hourly, that unless I could express the religious feeling. . . I would stop work and retire."[29]

She brought this challenge to the World War II Triptychs. She knew her Bible and quoted from it on many of them, noting on several the location of the passage in the Bible. An interesting aspect of her designs is her knowledge of Christian symbolism, from the very Catholic Saints in her "Angels of Victory" to her rather un-Protestant use of the Madonna and Child in others. Similarly, her use of a Heavenly Host of angels, her inclusion of the Doves of the Holy Spirit, and a representation of the cross in various guises, can probably be attributed to her close study of Early Renaissance paintings on her travels to Italy, or a carry-over from her early practice of the Episcopal Faith. The Christian Science faith is without symbolism or ritual instruments of any kind. Oakley offered her artistry to the Christian Science Monitor and other Church publications, but as Bailey Van Horn points out in her recently published biography of the artist, Oakley had several of her offerings turned down because trustees of the will of Mary Baker Eddy felt she would not have approved the artistic symbolism.[30]

The World War II triptychs are the least well-known of Violet Oakley's prodigious artistic *oeuvre*. Each one is represented by a four-color glass plate in the AAR records, in which a mass of administrative material is also included. CCAN records contain a black and white photograph of each of the triptychs, except for that of "David and Goliath." In the Papers of Violet Oakley, there are photographs of presentation ceremonies and a folder of notes and rough drawings showing how Oakley conceived and modified her designs.

In artistic presentation and spiritual content, these triptychs rank with Oakley's greatest murals, the ones created for the Pennsylvania State Capitol. In these small donations intended to bolster the war effort and urge it to victory, she was able to create a sub-text of hope for peace and the need for a spiritual attitude toward its achievement. These are art works in miniature in comparison to the Capitol murals. But they are artistic jewels in the Renaissance tradition.

IV.

Timeline

Between 1942 and 1945, Violet Oakley was commissioned by the CCAN to paint twenty-five altar-pieces for use in chapels on military bases and on warships. She was one of many artists to participate in this program. Several of her triptychs received national publicity and were exhibited at the Corcoran Gallery in Washington D.C.; Woodmere Art Gallery, Philadelphia, December 1943 through January 1944; The National Academy of Design, October 1945; and at the Headquarters of the Citizens Committee for the Army and Navy at 36 E. 36th Street, New York, NY, September 1945.

A control number was assigned to each triptych by the CCAN, sequentially for the over 300 completed and assigned works. Following is its record of triptychs painted by Violet Oakley.

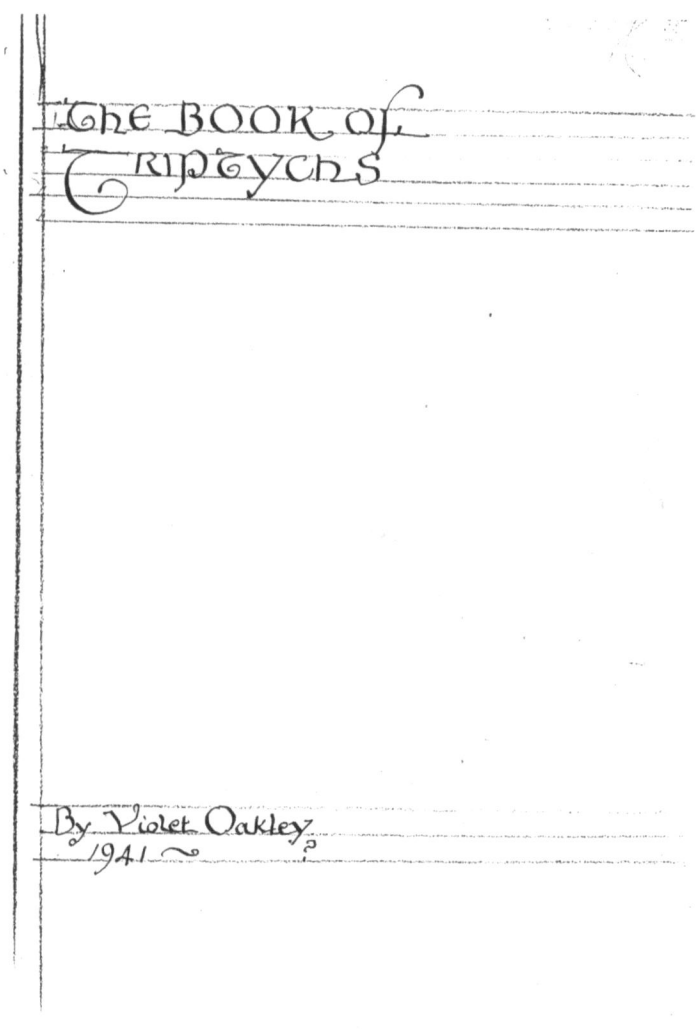

The BOOK of
TRIPTYCHS

By Violet Oakley
1941

Title page of the record Oakley kept
with pertinent information about each Triptych.

1941

Oakley began "The Book of Triptychs" and started painting them.

1942

The CCAN began distributing her triptychs.

The Angels of Victory (Triptych No. 5)

Oil on wood. Floyd Bennett Field, Long Island, February 13,1942-June 6,1946. Transferred to Milton (sic) Horwitz, May 12, 1974. Donated to the Delaware Art Museum by Joseph Flom and Martin Horwitz, 1975.

It remains in the DAR Collections, DAM #1975.129.

"An Altar-Piece for the Navy by Violet Oakley." *Philadelphia Inquirer*, March, 1942. With illustration.

Exhibition at the Delaware Art Museum, February 8 - May 25, 2014: "Blessed Are The Peacemakers": Violet Oakley's The Angels of Victory.

Christ Stilling the Storm (Triptych No. 23)

Oil on wood. USS Seattle (Midshipman's School, NYC), May 5, 1942-January 1944. Transferred to Floyd Bennett Field, NY, January 1944-June 6,

1946. Transferred to Milton (sic) Horwitz, May 12,1974. Present location unknown.

October 18, 1942, Article in *The New York Times Magazine.*

Madonna of the Crusaders (Triptych No. 42)

Oil on wood. Fort Dix, NJ, September 10, 1942-June 3,1946. Transferred to Camp George Jordan, Seattle, WA, December 18, 1946-September 23, 1949. Transferred September 23,1949 to Chapel-by-the-Sea, Fort Lawton, WA. I had no response to query letter. Present location unknown.

1943

Madonna of the Sea (Triptych No. 77)

Oil on wood. US Naval Hospital, St. Albans, NY, April 26, 1943. Transferred to US Naval Training Station, Sampson, NY, May 1943-October 2,1946. Transferred to US Naval Academy, Annapolis, MD, February 5,1959. Letters to the Command Chaplain and the Executive Director of the Museum indicated that this triptych had not been seen at the Naval Academy for over forty years. Present location unknown.

Madonna of the Sea (Triptych No. 111)

Oil on metal. USS Leedstown, September 9, 1943. It was welded to the
bulkhead in the Mess Hall to become a fixture of the ship.

Present location unknown.

The Angels of Victory (Triptych No.112)

Oil on wood. Camp Breckinridge, KY, August 3, 1943-December 19, 1946.

Transferred to Milton (sic) Horwitz May 12, 1974.

Present location unknown.

The Widow of Nain (Triptych No. 145)

Oil on metal. USS Langley, August 9, 1943. Transferred to USS Norfolk,
August 13, 1958. Article in *The Philadelphia Inquirer*, April 25, 1943.

Present location unknown.

1944

Madonna of the Sea (Triptych No. 137)

Oil on wood. US Naval Hospital, St. Albans, NY.

Present location unknown.

Christ Walking on Water (Triptych No. 144)

Oil on metal. USS Pennsylvania, December 7, 1944-April 1, 1946.

Transferred to St. John's Church, Little Silver, NJ.

Present location unknown.

Madonna of the Sea (Triptych No. 165)

Oil on metal. USS Baltimore , September 8, 1944. Transferred to NY Gospel

Misson to the Jews to December 10, 1946. Transferred to Milton (sic)

Horwitz, May 12, 1974. Donated to the William Benton Museum of Art,

University of Connecticut, Storrs, on Dec. 20 1978 by Martin Horwitz and

Joseph Flom, Accession No. 1978.20.2.

The Widow of Nain (Triptych No. 166)

Oil on wood. US Naval Hospital, Portsmouth,VA, October 2, 1944.

Transferred to US Naval Hospital, Norfolk, VA, February 3, 1960.

(Permanently installed on the walls of their Chapel).

This has not been confirmed.

Christ Stilling the Storm (Triptych No. 189)

Oil on metal. USS Massachusetts, July 27, 1944. Stored aboard April 30, 1946. Present location unknown.

Madonna of the Sea (Triptych No. 198)

Oil on metal. USS Currituck, April 11, 1944-July 8, 1947. Transferred to Milton (sic) Horwitz, May 12, 1974.
Present location unknown.

Christ Walking on the Water (Triptych No. 242)

Oil on metal. USS Cebu, May 4, 1944-November 19, 1947. Transferred to Milton (sic) Horwitz, May 12, 1974. Donated to the Philadelphia Museum of Art by Joseph Flom and Martin Horwitz, 1975. Accession #1975.180.1. On Exhibition in "A Grand Vision. Violet Oakley and the American Renaissance," Woodmere Art Museum, Chestnut Hill, PA, September 2017-January 2018.

1945

Madonna of the Crusaders (Triptych No. 197)

Oil on wood. 220th Field Artillery Group [Bar Harbor?], June 22, 1945-July 10, 1946. Transferred to Milton (sic) Horwitz, May 12, 1974. Present location unknown.

David and Goliath (Triptych No. 250)

Oil on wood. Indiantown Gap Military Reservation, PA, October 30, 1945-May 21, 1946. Transferred to Milton (sic) Horwitz, May 12, 1974. Present location unknown.

Christ the Carpenter (Triptych No. 253)

Oil on wood. Navy Yard Base Chapel, 4th Naval District, Philadelphia, PA, December 30, 1945. This triptych was designed to hang over the main altar at the Chapel of the Philadelphia Naval Base, which was finally closed in 1995. Although the Historic Buildings of the Base are now open to the public, the caption for a drawing of Christ in this triptych, included in the 2018 Oakley Exhibition at the Woodmere Art Museum indicated that the present location of the Triptych itself is unknown.[31]

The Widow of Nain (Triptych No. 277)

Oil on wood. Kennedy General Hospital, Memphis, TN, 1945.

Present location unknown.

Christ at the Pool of Bethesda (Triptych No. 279)

Oil on wood. Bethesda Naval Hospital, Bethesda, MD, 1945. This triptych is still located in a niche in the foyer of the Chapel of the Bethesda Naval Hospital. U.S. Navy Art Collection, Department of the Navy, Bethesda, MD. Highlight of the Exhibition "Violet Oakley's Spirit of History: 1895-1961." The Lore Degenstein Gallery, Susquehanna, PA, 2005, curated by Jane DuPree Richardson.

Madonna of the Ship (Triptych No. 308)

Oil on wood. The USS Nashville, 1945. Present location unknown.

1960

Christ Stilling the Storm (Triptych No. 141)

Oil on wood. The Merchant Marine Academy, Kings Point, NY, January 19, 1960) Present location unknown.

1964

Christ Stilling the Storm (Triptych No.309)

Oil on metal. (Completed by Edith Emerson following Oakley's death). At the 5th Naval District, Norfolk, VA Museum. To Milton (sic) Horwitz, May 12, 1974. Present location unknown.

1966

Title Unknown (Triptych No. 310)

Oil on wood. US Naval Hospital, Newport, RI. Church of the Good Shepherd, Plainview, NY, October 11, 1966. Present location unknown.

1974

The Widow of Nain (Triptych No. 374)

Oil on wood. (Completed by Edith Emerson following Oakley's death). To Milton (sic) Horwitz, May 12, 1974. This triptych was made rectangular, to be hung. Present location unknown.

Selected Bibliography

Primary Sources

The American Academy in Rome, Records. Archives of American Art, Smithsonian Institution, Washington, DC.

The Citizens Committee for the Army and Navy, Inc., Records 1940-1945. Archives of American Art, Smithsonian Institution, Washington, DC.

The Violet Oakley Papers, 1841-1981. Archives of American Art, Smithsonian Institution, Washington, DC. Reel 1272.

General

Beckwith, John. *Early Medieval Art*. New York, NY: Praeger Publishers, 1969. 178-180.

Blum, Shirley Neilsen. *Early Netherlandish Triptychs; a study in patronage*. Berkeley, CA: University of California Press, 1969.

Carter, Alice. *The Red Rose Girls: an uncommon story of art and love.* New York,NY: Harry N. Abrams, Publishers, 2000.

Daly, Gay. *Pre-Raphaelites in Love.* New York, NY: Tichnor & Fields, 1989.

Eddy, Mary Baker. *Church Manual of the First Church of Christ Scientist, in Boston, Mass.* Boston, U.S.A.: The Christian Science Publishing Society, 1920.

Ivey, Paul Eli. *Prayers in Stone: Christian Science Architecture in the United States, 1894-1930.* Urbana, IL: University of Illinois Press, 1999.

Likos, Patricia. "Violet Oakley: Lady Mural Painter." *Pennsylvania Heritage,* Fall 1988,14-21.

Mills, Sally. *Violet Oakley: The Decoration of the Alumnae House Living Room.* Poughkeepsie, NY: Vassar College Art Gallery, 1984.

_____. "What the Triptych Means. The Vassar Art of Violet Oakley." *Vassar Quarterly.* LXXX, No. 3 (Spring, 1984). 23-25.

Moss, Roger W. *Historic Sacred Places of Philadelphia.* Photographs by Tom Crane. Philadelphia, PA: University of Pennsylvania Press / A Barra Foundation Book, 2005. 102-5, 268, 271.

Pennsylvania Capitol Preservation Committee. *A Sacred Challenge: Violet Oakley and the Pennsylvania Capitol.* Harrisburg, PA: The Pennsylvania Capitol Preservation Committee, 2003.

Ricci, Patricia Likos. "Violet Oakley: American Renaissance Woman," *The Pennsylvania Magazine of History and Biography,*Vol. CXXVI, No. 2 (April 2002), [217]-248.

Rubinstein, Charlotte Streifer. *American Women Artists from Early Indian Times to the Present.* New York, NY: Avon Books, 1982. Violet Oakley, 159-161.

Van Horn, Bailey. *Violet Oakley: An Artist's Life.* Newark, NJ: University of Delaware Press, 2016. "Triptychs, 1940-1946," 351-354; "Appendix 3. List of Violet Oakley's World War II Altarpieces, 383-[386]; Illustrations, xiii.

Woods, Ellen N. "Higher Calling," *Military Officer Magazine.* September 2006. 100-105, 110.

World War II Triptychs

"An Altar-Piece for the Navy by Violet Oakley." *Philadelphia Inquirer,* March, 1942. Illustrated withTriptych No. 23, "Christ Stilling the Storm."

Bartlett, Arthur. "Church Goes to GI Joe." Included in CCAN Records. Name and date of publication not included.

Grills, Matt. "For God & Country," *The American Legion Magazine.* Vol. 159, No. 6 (December 2005), 22-24, 26-28.

"An Exhibition of Triptychs or Devotional Pictures for the Armed Forces." Sponsored by the Citizens Committee for the Army and Navy at the National Academy of Design, October 10-23, 1942.

"Exhibition of Triptych Altarpieces, painted for the Armed Forces of the United States by well-known artists. Loaned by the CCAN. December 12, 1943-January 2, 1944. The Woodmere Art Gallery, Chestnut Hill, Pa. (Included Oakley's "The Madonna of the Sea," "Christ Walking on the Sea," and "The Compassionate Christ Raising the Son of the Widow of Nain".)

McCullough, Mark M., Chaplain, USA-Ret. "Religion in the Civil War," Talk given to the Susquehanna Civil War Round Table, Sunbury, PA, 26 October 2006.

Mechlin, Leila. "The Art World: Triptychs, Contemporary Religious Paintings for the Army and Navy." *The Evening Star.* Washington, DC, 14 January 1945. (Mentions Violet Oakley.)

Morgan, Hallowell V. "The Triptych Movement." *The Philadelphia Forum,* Vol. XXIV, No. 4 (December 1944), 5, 24. (Illustrated with Triptych No. 23, "Christ Stilling the Storm ".)

Morgan, Mrs. Junius S. "On the Altars of Freedom." *THINK Magazine.* December 1943.

Reed, George L., Chaplain COL, USA-Ret. Personal Interview, Vevay, IN, 20 April 2009.

"Religious Army Art." *The Art Digest,* New York, N.Y., October 15, 1942. (Mentions Violet Oakley.)

Ricci, Patricia Likos, Guest Curator. *A Grand Vision: Violet Oakley and the American Renaissance.* Chestnut Hill, PA: Woodmere Art Museum, 2017.

Richardson, Jane DuPree. "Violet Oakley: Art, History, Spirituality," *Susquehanna Life.* Vol. 12, Issue 1 (Spring 2005). (Refers to Triptych No. 279, "The Pool of Bethesda," 30-31,43.)

Rinehart, Mary Roberts. "Altars at the War Fronts." *Bar Harbor Times.* Included in CCAN Records. Date of publication not noted.

Roosevelt, Eleanor. "My Day, January 6, 1945." United Features Syndicate, Inc., 1945. (Mentions the Corcoran Gallery exhibition.)

Tarkington, Booth. "The Twentieth Century Triptychs". *The Philadelphia Forum,* Vol. XXIV, No. 4 (December 1944), 4. (Illustrated with Triptych No. 23, "Christ Stilling the Storm".)

Thomas, Rear Admiral Wm. H., (ChC), USN. "Triptychs: Traditional Aid to Worship," *Shipmate Magazine,* U.S. Naval Academy Alumni Association, December, 1945. (Illustrated with an unidentified color image of one of Violet Oakley's "Madonna of the Sea" Triptychs.)

"Trip Exhibition," *The Evening Star,* 20 January, 1945. (A review of the Corcoran Gallery exhibition.)

Acknowledgements

I cannot thank the following people enough.

Dr. Valerie Livingston, former Head of the Art Department and Director of the Lore Degenstein Gallery at Susquehanna University, Selinsgrove, Pennsylvania. She gave me the job of curating the Violet Oakley Exhibition there. Also, the Gallery staff at the time of the Exhibition, Jody Horn, Judy Marvin, and Sarah Herlinger, who were helpful in so many ways and fun to work with.

Ruthann Hubbert-Kemper, former Executive Director of the Pennsylvania State Capitol Restoration Commission, who was always helpful with information about Violet Oakley and her work.

Capt. (CHC), USN J. Steven Evans, Director of Pastoral Care Services, the Bethesda Naval Hospital, Bethesda, MD, who was responsible for requesting The U.S. Navy Department to loan the Oakley triptych "Christ at the Pool of Bethesda" for the Lore Degenstein Gallery Exhibition.

Other professionals who were helpful along the way: Marshall Price at the National Academy of Design, New York City; Douglas Paschall at The Woodmere Art Museum, Chestnut Hill, PA; Mr. James Cheever, Curator of the U.S. Naval Academy Museum, Annapolis, MD.

Friends and neighbors:

Mary Ann and Bill Wren of Rockville, MD, who scouted the Bethesda Naval Hospital and found and photographed the Oakley triptych there.

Louisa Peat O'Neil of Rockville, MD, who accompanied me and the staff of the Lore Degenstein Gallery on our first visit to the Bethesda Naval Hospital to see the triptych and to photograph it from all directions, front and back. Peat also made the connection for me between the historic site of her great-uncle Dr. Tait O'Neil, M.D. and well-known sculptor of athletes and Violet Oakley, friends and artists together in Philadelphia.

Meredith Luhrs, artist and friend in Vevay, Indiana, with whom I had many discussions about the history of art and Oakley's place based on her World War II triptychs. It was a great learning experience.

The Staff of the Archives of American Art at the Smithsonian Institution, Washington, D.C., in particular Judy Therom, retired Head of

Reference, Marisa Burgoin, current Head of Reference, and, most recently, Craig Schiffert, AAA Rights and Reproductions, with whom I had a most interesting and informative meeting.

And to Kevin Begos, my son and publisher.

My thanks to you all.

Notes

[1] Citizens Committee for the Army and Navy, Inc. Records, 1940-1945. Archives of American Art, The Smithsonian Institution, Washington, D.C. NOTE: This is the correct title for this organization. The Air Force did not exist as a separate Department of the Armed Forces until after World War II. Up to and including WWII, it was under the administration of the Army and referred to as the Army Air Corps or the United States Army Air Force.

[2] Morgan, Hallowell V. "The Triptych Movement." *The Philadelphia Forum*, December 1945

[3] Thomas, RADM Wm. H., (CHC), USN. "Triptychs: Traditional Aid to Worship," *Shipmate Magazine*, U.S. Naval Academy Alumni Association, December 1945.

[4] Junius Spencer Morgan, Jr. was one of two sons of John Pierpont "Jack" Morgan, Jr., only son of J.P. Morgan. Junius was referred to as "Junior" to distinguish him from his great-grandfather and an older Junius Spencer Morgan, nephew of J.P. Morgan, who became the librarian of the Morgan Rare Book Library at Princeton University. Ardizzone, Heidi. *An Illuminated Life: Belle Da Costa Greene's Journey from Prejudice to Privilege.* New York, NY: W.W. Norton & Company, 2007. 80-81.

[5] Bartlett, Arthur. "Church Goes to GI Joe." Included in the CCAN Records, but name and date of publication not included.

[6] Barry Faulkner Papers, 1900-1973. Archives of American Art, The Smithsonian Institution, Washington, D.C.

[7] American Academy in Rome, Records. Archives of American Art, Smithsonian Institution, Washington, D.C.

[8] Rinehart, Mary Roberts. "Altars at the War Fronts. *Bar Harbor Times.* Included in the CCAN Records, date not included. Op. cit.

[9] Morgan, Mrs. Junius S. "On the Altars of Freedom." *THINK Magazine,* December 1943.

[10] AAR Records, op. cit.

[11] Morgan, Hallowell V., op. cit.

[12] AAR Records, p. cit.

[13] Beckwith, John. *Early Medieval Art.* New York, NY: Praeger Publishers, 1969 (c1964). 178-180.

[14] Blum, Shirley Neilson. *Early Netherlandish Triptychs; a study in patronage.* Berkeley, CA: University of California Press, 1969.

[15] Reed, George L., Chaplain COL, USA-Ret. Personal Interview, Vevay, IN, 20 April 2009. Initially, all chaplains were Protestant, as is COL. Reed.

[16] Today, over 200 religious organizations have been granted ecclesiastical endorsement by the Department of Defense, up from 10 in 1945. Protestants and Catholics make up the majority. The first Jewish chaplain served in 1862, when Congress amended the law that provided only for Christians. In 1987, the Department of Defense registered the Buddhist Churches of America as an ecclesiastical endorsing agency. In 1998, the recruitment of chaplains to serve Hindu soldiers was authorized. In 1999, the first Navy Muslim chaplain was assigned to the Marine Corps at Camp Pendleton. The free exercise of religious belief for all members of the military, including the right to hold no belief, is the foundation of today's military chaplaincy. Grills, Matt. "For God & Country." *The American Legion Magazine.* Vol. 159, No. 6 (December 2005), 26.

[17] Van Horn, Bailey. *Violet Oakley: An Artist's Life.* Newark, NJ: University of Delaware Press, 2016.

[18] The Women's International League for Peace and Freedom was founded in 1915 during World War I, with Jane Addams as its first president.

[19] Morgan, Hallowell V., op. cit., 24. The Philadelphia Triptych Committee cooperated with the national committee. Sponsors Included His Eminence Dennis Cardinal Dougherty, the Right Rev. Oliver J. Hart, Bishop Fred P. Corson, Rev. Rex S. Clements, Rev. Ivan Murray Rose, Dr.Abraham A. Neumann, Rear-Admiral Milo F. Draemel, USN, the Hon. George Wharton Pepper, Dr. Thomas S. Gates, Martin W. Clement, Philip C. Staples, J. Howard Pew, Howard A. Loeb, and John J. Sullivan, as well as fifty active committee members headed by Joshua Ash Pearson, chairman.

[20] Pennsylvania Capitol Preservation Committee. *A Sacred Challenge: Violet Oakley and the Pennsylvania Capitol.* Harrisburg, PA: The Pennsylvania Capitol Preservation Committee, 2003.

[21] Moss, Roger W. *Historic Sacred Places of Philadelphia.* Philadelphia, PA: University of Pennsylvania Press, 2005. 102-105.

[22] Moss, Roger W. *Historic Sacred Places of Philadelphia.* Philadelphia, PA: University of Pennsylvania Press, 2005. 102-105.

[23] Moss, Roger W. *Historic Sacred Places of Philadelphia.* Philadelphia, PA: University of Pennsylvania Press, 2005. 102-105.

[24] Ibid. 268-271.

[25] Daly, Gay. *Pre-Raphaelites in Love.* New York, NY: Tichnor & Fields, 1989.

[26] The Pennsylvania Shipyard. *National Register of Historic Sites.* National Park Service. Wikipedia.

[27] CCAN Records, Op. cit.

[28] Eddy, Mary Baker. *Church Manual of the First Church of Christ Scientist.* Boston, Mass.: The Christian Science Publishing Society, 1920.

[29] Likos, Patricia. *Violet Oakley: Lady Mural Painter.* Pennsylvania Heritage, Fall 1988, 14-21.

[30] Van Horn, Op. cit, 328.

[31] Ricci, Patricia Likos, Guest Curator. *A Grand Vision: Violet Oakley and the American Renaissance.* Chestnut Hill, PA: Woodmere Art Museum, 2017. 101, 105-106.